A FANTASY FEAST

A collection of my fantasy poems

Jen Elvy

To everyone who needs a touch of magic in their lives

CONTENTS

INTRODUCTION

Welcome to my second self published poetry collection. This book will transport you away from your everyday worries and give your imagination a feast of fantasy.

The first part of this book features my long narrrative poem, A Hunt for Sparkled Treasurses, which is currently available as an ebook. I always intended for it to be part of a larger collection. Many of you will be reading it for the first time, and some of you for the first time in paperback. I hope you enjoy reading it as much as I enjoyed writing it.

In the second part of this book you will find other poems that tell a story. Some are relatively short and others are longer. The poems are full of adventure and perfect as bedtime stories for children.

The third part of this book contains poems about fantasy characters and the fourth part contains poems about fantasy settings.

I hope you enjoy what I have to offer and feel free to let me know what you think by connecting with me on Social Media. Feel free, also, to use them as inspiration for your own creations, just as many of you have done with my other collection, The Perfect Prompt.

Happy reading,
Much love
Jen

Social Media

Here is where to find me:

Instagram: @jen.elvy_poems
Twitter: @Jen_poet31

Facebook: Jen's Poems
Pinterest: Jen.evly_writer

A HUNT FOR SPARKLED TREASURES

THE CASTLE

In crystal waters in the wood
An ancient, grey, stone castle stood.
It stood alone on an island so small,
And yet there it was, so proud and tall.
My friend and I had to go and look.
To cross the water, a boat we took.
In a tiny rowing boat, we paddled across
To the island, all covered in moss.
No one had dared to visit, it appeared.
We thought it'd been abandoned for years!
Can you imagine our surprise
When we saw it looked so different inside?
There were ladders and pipes and passageways.
My friend and I were in a daze.
Suddenly we saw upon a wall
A plaque so golden and so small.
A plaque that said, "Somewhere inside,
Several precious treasures reside;
The most valuable treasures ever seen,
And they are guarded by the queen!"

A SECRET PLACE

We had to go and find a queen
In the strangest castle we'd ever seen.
So we simply had to look around,
And see if royalty could be found.
Down that passage or up the ladder?
What if we were to find an adder?
But there was no sign of reptiles in here,
Though a twisty and strange looking pipe did appear!
It was green and yellow and bright to our eyes.
Should we go down it to find our prize?
Go down it we did, but the queen wasn't there.
Instead we were out in the open air!
We were on a sandy, golden beach,
With little rock pools within our reach.
Crabs and fishes dwelled within
The pools with water, sparkling.
Just then, to us, it suddenly occurred
We had arrived in an underworld!

THE TURQUOISE SEA

The underworld was quite the place!
Of human life there was no trace.
The turquoise water sparkled so!
For a swim we simply had to go!
The water was warm as we waded in.
It felt like silk upon our skin.
And so we swam along together;
I felt like I could swim forever.
The water was so blissful and calm,
Filled with a certain magical charm.
Suddenly a cottage came into sight,
With walls adorned in creamy white.
It stood on a beach of golden sand,
So quaint and lonely it did stand,
Just like a cottage from a fairy tale book.
We thought we would go and take a look.
Slowly and steadily we swam ashore.
So keen and so eager to see more.

THE COTTAGE

We slowly walked up to the little house.
All was silent, as quiet as a mouse.
We knocked upon the wooden door.
Was the cottage empty? Could we explore?
But then we heard footsteps coming our way.
The door opened slowly and, to our dismay,
A man stood there, unkempt and sleepy.
We took a step back as he looked a bit creepy.
"Welcome," he said. "Would you like to come in?"
On his face there appeared a wide, toothy grin.
We looked at each other with fear and confusion;
We suddenly felt threatened by our seclusion.
But the man let us in and all seemed fine.
The man spoke slowly and in rhyme.
"I know about the jewels, I'll tell you so.
They were hidden in a cave a long time ago.
There is, alas, a long way to travel,
And there are tricky clues to unravel."
We thanked the man and went on our way.
We needed more clues without delay.

THE QUEEN

"Many clues to unravel," the man said;
A million thoughts raced around my head.
In the end we decided, "To the castle we must go
To see the only one who would know."
We travelled back across the shore
And swam the warm, calm ocean once more.
We found the pipe that led us to the beach,
And, thankfully, it was just within our reach.
So we clambered up and up until
We reached a room that stopped us still.
There sat the lady we needed, the queen;
The most formidable figure we'd ever seen.
Dressed in pink with a lion by her side,
Her throne was as white as a dress for a bride.
At first she denied all knowledge of the jewels,
But we knew she wasn't abiding by the rules.
When asked again, at last she relented,
Although to send us away she was tempted.
She told us to look for a faraway cave,
Its shape is familiar, but also strange.
We bowed to the queen and thanked her so
And off on our search we had to go.

OBSTACLES

We slid down the pipe to the beach once more.
Now we knew what we were searching for;
A cave with a familiar, yet strange shape.
We hoped we wouldn't get into a scrape.
Suddenly we came to a puddle so deep.
It was muddy and swampy, with leaves in a heap.
There seemed to be no way of getting across.
When suddenly, out from under the moss
Came a curious winged creature. Maybe he could help.
He pointed to his wings and gave a loud yelp.
And then to our surprise, his wings transferred to us!
We thanked him most kindly, but he wanted no fuss.
Before long we came to a wall so high.
Our wings had gone now, so we couldn't fly.
No space underneath and we couldn't reach the top.
It seemed that our journey had come to a stop.
All hopes were dashed, our wishes denied.
My friend was in tears. "Please move, wall!" he cried.
And then our despair turned into dismay,
As the wall said simply, "Why didn't you say?"
The wall shrank lower and lower and then
We were ready to continue our journey again.

THE GUARD

Soon we could tell we were getting close.
We came across an iron gate post
With a grand iron gate so huge; so tall.
We couldn't push it open; not at all.
"What are you doing?" said a very stern voice.
We stopped pushing then; we had no choice.
A fierce looking guard was standing there.
He gave us a very angry glare.
We knew we needed to go through the gate
Straight away; there was no time to wait.
We asked, but the guard said, "On your way!
You have no business here; go away!"
"So what now?" we thought. "Should we plead?
Should we promise to do a good deed?
We could fight but we have no sword
And that would bring us no reward."
Suddenly, my friend touched his head.
"I have a great idea," he said.
"We need to put the guard to sleep
And then through the gate we can creep.
We'll check his pockets; we'll seize his keys.
Oh it will be such a breeze!"
"Yes!" I said. "We'll do it now!"
But the real question would be, "How?"

THROUGH THE GATE

We had a wander and what did we find?
A stall selling medicine of every kind.
We bought a potion and returned to the guard.
Giving him the medicine wasn't very hard.
"Have a sip of this, it's nice," we said.
He sipped it and yawned, "I want my bed!"
He fell into a very deep sleep
And into his pockets, we had a peep.
There was the key, so shiny and gold.
We unlocked the gate, and through it we strolled.
We walked for a while and there we saw
A sight we'd never seen before;
An enormous cave stood before us,
Shaped like the mouth of a hippopotamus.
It was indeed strange yet so familiar.
And also familiar was the figure
That stood there, dressed in emerald green.
Yes, the figure was the queen!

THE CAVE

Yes, in the entrance stood the queen.
Through a passageway, she had been.
The castle was on the other side.
It seemed she'd taken us for a ride.
She'd led us down a path so wrong,
When we were nearly there all along.
We were furious and demanded the jewels.
The queen said, "You are not playing by the rules!"
Then she led us into the cave so dark,
Where a group of fireflies gave only a spark.
Soon we came to a very large room;
Away, it seemed, from the darkened gloom.
The room was lit with a bright red flame.
Here, we saw exactly why we came.
The queen led us to a wooden chest.
To hide our excitement, we did our best.
The queen opened it with a deafening creak;
And then we froze, unable to speak.
For there in front of us (and the queen)
Were the most precious jewels we'd ever seen.

THE JEWELS

We stared at the jewels for what seemed an hour.
For we were clearly under their power.
"Would you like to keep them?" the queen teased.
She really wanted us down on our knees!
"Well, would you?" the queen sternly said.
Still dumbfounded, we nodded our heads.
"If you want to, " she said "You can, however,
You'll both have to be my servants forever."
The thought seemed too much for us to bear,
But we couldn't just leave the treasure there.
We'd travelled so far and done so much
And at last, the jewels were within our touch.
We had some time to think this through
And we wondered, what we could do?
"Should we try to run off with the treasure?"
"No that's wrong; it would bring no pleasure."
"Then we are stuck here forever, aren't we?"
"Not so fast, just follow me..."
My friend, he bravely took the lead.
Headstrong he was, determined to succeed.
He told the queen that if we could keep ten
Then she'll never have to see us again.
"No way!" said the queen. "You'll keep just two."
My friend and I shrugged; that would have to do.
We were lucky enough to have two of them.
We picked a sparkling diamond and a purple gem.
We thanked the queen kindly and went on our way,
Hoping to go back for more jewels one day.

MORE POETIC TALES

THE PRINCESS AND THE FOREST

There was once a young princess, it is little known
Who entered a forest all on her own.
Can you imagine her look of surprise
When the forest turned purple before her eyes?
She looked all around at the purple glow,
Wondering how much further she should go.
Perhaps she should turn back, the queen would worry.
But I could go further, she thought, if I hurry.
So on went the princess through the purple trees,
When something so beautiful brought her to her knees.
A woodland clearing full of wild, purple flowers;
She felt she could sit in this space for hours,
Picking lots of bunches for everyone she knew.
But there was no time. She knew what she should do.
She turned around and ran back home,
Vowing that soon, the purple forest, she would roam.

All the next day the princess felt glum.
No one could comfort her, not even her mum.
The very next morning, she rushed to the door.
She just had to visit the forest once more.
While her mother and father sat and drank tea,
She opened the door oh so quietly.
She rushed down the path as fast as she could,
So very impatient to see the purple wood.
When she reached the forest, she came to a halt.
She turned round to check she hadn't been caught.
All was clear so she slowly wandered in.
As the forest turned purple, she gave a huge grin.
She walked on until she saw something on the ground,
Glinting in the sunlight, waiting to be found.
As she knelt down, she spied two brass keys,
Laying on a purple cloth, begging to be seized.

The princess regarded the keys carefully.
She saw them gleaming so perfectly.
She picked them up with a gentle hand,
Feeling like the luckiest girl in the land.
Should she turn back now or should she go on?

Had her parents realised that she was gone?
She decided she'd carry on a little longer.
Her resolve, it seemed, was never stronger.
Soon the sound of big buzzing bees
Drew her attention to a group of trees.
In two of the tree trunks she noticed a door.
Could this be what the keys were for?
She carefully crept to the first of the trees,
Put a key in the door, and it opened with ease.
And there she saw, inside this forest tree,
The prettiest dress she ever did see.

It was purple, of course, with frills and pearls;
Just the sort of thing for royal little girls.
The princess tried it on and, to her delight,
It just so happened that it fit her just right.
"Oh what a pretty dress! See how it glimmers!"
She said; and she added "I must find a mirror!"
There were none inside the tree trunk she was in,
But the princess knew just where to begin.
The second key, she still had in her hand
And she put it in the second door, as planned.
Not only did she find a mirror in there,
But lots of shiny purple jewels for her hair,
A purple diamond necklace and a purple crown.
She'd be the purplest little princess in the town.
When she put it all on, she looked glamorous indeed.
She had all the purple prettiness a princess should need.

WOODEN WINTER HUT

I took a walk on a winter's night.
The snow was sparkling in the moonlight.
The air was crisp and the trees were still.
I trekked my way across the field until
I came to some trees and beyond them I saw
Something that I simply could not ignore;
A little wooden hut with fairy lights all round
And when I got closer, guess what I found?
Footprints leading to the small wooden door
And the lights casting shadows on the forest floor.
I started to ponder this magical sight
That stood before me on a winter's night.
Who lives in this hut? Are they inside?
Is it a resting place? Or where they reside?
A million questions entered my mind
And the answers I truly wanted to find.

WOODEN WINTER HUT II

The hut, it seemed, was a resting place
For a wizard with a friendly face.
I bravely knocked on the wooden door,
And then heard creaking on the wooden floor.
The door slowly opened and there the wizard stood,
Holding in his arms a bundle of firewood.
We stood there for a moment; neither of us spoke.
I couldn't help staring at his wonderful cloak.
It was captivating, colourful, unlike any I knew;
I wouldn't have been surprised if it was magical too!
"Can I help you?" the wizard said with a smile.
"You look as though you've walked a fair mile."
I looked beyond him and into the hut.
There was a fireplace and a bowl of chestnuts.
I was desperate to go and rest my weary legs.
I did not want to seem rude and beg.
But the wizard seemed to read my mind.
"Would you like to come in?" His voice was so kind.
So we sat and chatted long into the night
And we snacked on roasted chestnuts till the morning light.

THE FAIRY QUEEN AND THE GOLDEN POND

'Twas a warm spring day by the fairy pool.
Butterflies fluttered by, trying to keep cool.
Bubbles and birds flew around in the breeze;
Elves and fairies were doing as they pleased.

When suddenly, from down below,
There came a yellow-orange glow.
The light shone big and bright and bold
And then the pond lit up with gold.

The water bubbled and out from the pond,
Slowly rose a throne and a fairy with a wand;
The most beautiful fairy they had ever seen,
The formidable, elegant fairy queen.

All was silent as she rose further up;
As she sipped fruit tea from a golden cup.
She commanded attention when, at last, she spoke
And her royal black feline, she started to stroke.

She told all the creatures and fairies and elves
That they needed at once to defend themselves.
There were forces of evil at work in the land;
As a team they would all need to make a stand.

So everyone chattered long into the night
About how they'd combat this dreadful plight.
And finally they came up with a brilliant plan;
A plan that would help them defend their land.

Together they would all make a potion.
Together they would all cause commotion.
Together they would stop evil from winning;
Together they all just couldn't stop grinning.

Then appeared an ugly troll, who said,
"I'm the master; now, bow your head."
The fairy team was well prepared
And therefore nobody was scared.

They made their potion and gave it to the master.
As they waited, they willed it to work faster.
Suddenly the master fell to his knees
And the folk around him began to sneeze.

A commotion was made; the battle was won.
All the team celebrated by the evening sun.
And as for the master and all of his men,
They went away in shame and were never seen again.

THE WIZARD

The wizard lives at the top of a hill
That no one can climb of their own free will.
You call for the wizard and he guides you up
With a sip of drink from his magical cup.
One day I needed the wizard's assistance
To reverse a spell that required persistence.
So I wandered the village till I came to the hill
That no one could climb of their own free will.
I shouted for the wizard and he came.
As fairy tale wizards, he was just the same,
With a wispy white beard and a starry cloak;
He appeared to me in a dense fog of smoke.
He passed me the cup and the drink I sipped
And I gave a gasp as backwards I tipped,
And a force pulled me up and up until
I found myself at the top of the hill.
Into the wizard's house I wandered.
"Where did he disappear to?" I pondered.
With anticipation I began to quiver,
As, before me, I saw a miniature river.
There were vines on the wall and little birds tweeting.
I wondered what I'd get by way of a greeting.
The corridor was dark as I climbed some stairs.
Then I saw, in a doorway, a room with two chairs;
There was the wizard, who bowed and then said,
"Take a seat, child and bow your head."
I did as I was told and the wizard made a spell
To retrieve my key from down the well.
With a flash and the sound of a loud brass band,
The golden key appeared in my hand.
I solemnly thanked him and promised him so,
To the witch and her well, I would nevermore go.

FAIRIES IN MY BEDROOM

I walked into my bedroom
And what did I see?
A fairy who was reading
A bedtime story.

Another fairy was in my bed,
All tucked up cosy and warm,
While her friend read a little tale
Of a wild and windy storm.

I stared at them and listened,
Not believing my ears nor my eyes,
Was the fairy enjoying the story?
Would the ending be a surprise?

But the fairies didn't realise
That I was even there.
I wondered if I should go over
And fetch my teddy bear.

But still the fairy continued
Her story, whispering gently,
While her friend lay wide awake,
Listening intently.

I turned and tiptoed out of the room,
Quietly closing the door.
I wanted to know where those fairies lived
And if I could find any more.

THE PLAN

A plan was hatched in a grotto one day
To try to frighten the goblins away.
Those fearsome creatures were at it again,
Trying to make it eternally rain!
The elves and fairies; they knew what to do;
They needed to form one big solid crew,
"To stick together through thick and through thin;
Make sure the gruesome goblins never win."
So in the grotto, in the dead of night,
They decided to give the goblins a fright,
To teach them a lesson they'd never forget,
A plan that would be their cleverest yet.
They raided their cupboards; they searched their shelves,
Made costumes to dress up as goblins themselves.
They said to the goblins,"We'll do what you say."
But just when the goblins thought they had their way,
The fairies and elves, to suit their own gain,
Cast the spell backwards so it would NEVER rain.
The sun, it would now shine forever more.
The goblins cowered and fell to the floor.

RIVER WATER CHARMS

The ancient path
I walk along,
As daybreak sings
Its soft, sweet song.

The twinkling charms
I have to find.
Please, dear river,
Please be kind.

As I reach
The sparkling waters,
I'm aware I'm near
The witch's quarters.

So softly, gently
I must tread
Or the witch
Will have me dead.

The pool reflects
My fearful face.
Of hope or joy,
There is no trace.

But this risk
I have to take.
My sweet fortune
I must make.

I reach across;
I will get wet
But the charms
I have to get.

I bend down;
I dip my hand
But all I feel
Is soggy sand.

Alas, the charm
I thought I saw
Was just a sunbeam
On the water pure.

THE WISHING TREE

"What will you wish for?"
My friend said to me,
As soon as we reached
The wishing tree.

"Can you wish," she said,
"To be the queen?"
"I'm not sure," I said.
"I'm not too keen.

I want to wish
For a horse so white
That will watch me
When I sleep at night."

"I'll wish," she said,
"For it always to be spring."
"But think of the fun
That winter can bring!"

"Maybe," she said,
With a little smile,
"I'll just ask to go
Somewhere sunny for a while."

I stood there as she
Continued to ponder,
For so long, my mind
Began to wander.

Until, at last,
She made her choice,
With such excitement
In her voice;

"I know!" she said.
"I'll ask for a throne
And a wishing tree
Of my very own."

BUSTER

A dragon appeared in my bedroom one day.
He came to the window and said, "Can I stay?"
He was no bigger than a box of toys
And he said he was friendly to girls and boys.
So I let him stay. How could I not,
When he promised he'd magic me a great big yacht?
I made him a den in a box, with some straw
And told him to promise not to roar.
He told me he couldn't roar or breathe fire
But he said that he was a really good flyer.
"In that case," I said, "take me for a ride."
So he shrank me down and we flew outside.
So there I was on a magic dragon's back,
When suddenly I found myself under attack.
Some funny creatures were firing balls at me.
I lost my balance as one hit my knee.
But just as I thought I would fall to the ground,
I heard a kind of rumbling sound.
My dragon was trying to roar, it seemed.
The funny creatures looked and screamed.
I thought they were goblins, but I couldn't quite see.
Before I knew it I was being pulled to safety.
The dragon tugged at me with all the strength he could muster
And that was when I thought to name him Buster.
Now he is my hero, so little but so strong!
With Buster by my side, I can't go wrong.

A FAIRY ADVENTURE

Outside a little house,
In a deep dark wood,
Elegant and dainty,
A little fairy stood.

As I got closer,
She asked me my name.
She sprinkled fairy dust
So our sizes were the same.

She then ran away
And I followed after.
As I approached,
I could hear her laughter.

When I caught up,
She whispered to me,
"I live over there,
In that little tree."

So off we went
To her fairy house
And there we saw
A tiny fairy mouse.

"His name is Timmy,"
She said to me,
And then she said,
"Will you stay for tea?"

So we ate fairy cakes
And strawberry ice cream.
We chatted for hours;
It felt like a dream.

But just when I was
Having such fun,
She said, "Look at the time,
You must run."

She magicked me back
To my normal size.
When she opened the door
I couldn't believe my eyes

I was back home
In my very own room.
I hope I have another
Fairy adventure soon.

DREAM

Last night I had a funny dream
About a forest with a stream.
I stood next to a spiny tree
And saw a strange man next to me.
He wore a hat; he had a beard,
And what he'd say, I deeply feared.
But there was no need for alarm;
For when he spoke, he had such charm.
He had a squeaky, tinny voice.
He said, "We won, now let's rejoice!"
Before I could ask what he meant,
He led me to a tiny tent.
He grinned at me, then went inside.
I wondered, did he want to hide?
He took a while, I grew quite bored;
Felt that I was being ignored.
Eventually, out he did come.
In his hand was a tiny drum.
When I asked him, "What is that for?"
He simply grinned at me once more.
Suddenly, he began to fade.
All things around me softly swayed.
It seemed, alas, my dream was done.
I never found out what I'd won.

THE BIRD SPELL

There once was a wizard who made a spell
To make his apprentice rich, fair and well.
But the spell went quite wrong; it was absurd;
It actually turned him into a bird!
Imagine the people; Oh how they laughed
When they saw him sitting in a bird bath!
How on earth could a spell have gone so wrong?
The wizard said, "Maybe it was too long."
He flicked frantically through his big spell book
And suddenly shouted, "I've got it! Look!
To remove this strange spell, I'll need some things,
A box of matches and a ball of string,
A toy for a cat, a slice of cake,
A teacher's whistle and a garden rake."
The people lent a hand; they got the stuff.
The wizard just hoped it was good enough.
The apprentice flapped his wings a few times;
The bells in the clock tower gave three chimes.
The apprentice gave a big squawk and then
He was back to his old self once again.
"Thank you all so much!" he loudly exclaimed.
"I don't need money and I don't need fame.
I'm just happy to be back to myself.
I'd sooner be me than have fame or wealth."

THE MERMAID AND THE UNICORN I

Part 1 - A Problem at the Lake

The mermaid and the unicorn lived on a silver lake.
One day the mermaid made the most dreadful mistake.
"What kind of mistake was that?" I hear you loudly cry.
She let the silver lake run so completely dry.
"How," you may ask, "did she do a thing like that?"
It was the work of a magical, malicious hat.
A wily old wizard, about a hundred years old,
Told her that the hat would fill up with gold.
"Just put it on the bottom of the lake," he said;
And, without another word, he turned and fled.
But instead of making them as rich as can be,
It dried up the lake, leaving Unicorn thirsty.
So what to do now they were in such a mess?
It'd take more to solve this than a pretty mermaid dress.
The wizard, of course, was nowhere to be seen.
To undo this magic, he would not be keen.
They would have to find someone else to assist.
But suddenly around them was a dull grey mist.
A voice spoke, "To fill up this lake you will need
To tell the queen of unicorns you're sorry for your greed."
But where would they find this unicorn queen?
"In the silver castle right by the stream."
So off they went to find the queen of unicorns,
The mermaid filled with guilt and her friend so forlorn.

THE MERMAID AND THE UNICORN II

Part 2 - To the Castle

The castle looked ever so grand and tall.
Its silver walls glistened like a glitter ball.
A drawbridge opened upon their arrival.
This visit was as vital as their own survival.
They crossed the drawbridge so tentatively,
The mermaid, so glum, and Unicorn, still thirsty.
They made their way in and what did they find?
A unicorn with a face so gentle and so kind.
But there was a lady by the unicorn's side
Whose face made the mermaid want to run and hide.
She was elegant and fancy and dressed like a queen.
The look on her face was so fierce and so mean.
"I'm here to say sorry," the mermaid softly said.
The queen simply frowned and shook her head.
"I was ever so greedy," the mermaid went on.
But still the queen glowered. This was going so wrong!
The mermaid went on to say what she'd done.
As she spoke every word, she just wanted to run.
The queen was furious with the mermaid's tale.
She said it was the worst kind of unicorn betrayal.
The mermaid cried and begged to be forgiven.
The queen admitted she was brave for her admission.
Said the queen, "Very well I will grant you this,
It seems like, the unicorn, a drink he does miss.
I will fill the lake up with a magical pail
So long as my daughter can have your mermaid tail."
The mermaid, she had to accept her cruel fate
And fill up the lake before it was too late.
So the lake was now filled with silver water once more
And Unicorn could have a fresh drink like before.

THE MERMAID AND THE UNICORN III

Part 3 - The Mermaid's Tail

The princess loved her new mermaid tail.
"I miss it so much!" the mermaid would wail.
And now if you'd care to cast your mind
To the royal unicorn, so gentle and kind.
The unicorn was the princess's best friend;
Only on the unicorn could she depend.
She could understand what he wanted to say
And all day long, together, they would play.
The unicorn often heard the mermaid's cries
And to the princess, he could tell no lies.
He told the princess how much the tail was missed,
Only to be well and truly dismissed.
"I will not give it up!" The princess stomped her feet.
The mermaid felt glum and so very incomplete.
The princess visited her at the silver lake.
She said, "Maybe I'm making a huge mistake,
But I'll give your tail back with every last scale
If you promise to make me my very own tail."
The mermaid happily agreed to the deal
And, from her pocket, she produced a colour wheel.
She'd make the princess a tail, so unique,
With colours so enchanting; it would only take a week!
So one whole week later, the tail was complete.
The mermaid was feeling so much more upbeat.
She strode to the castle, her head held high.
The princess gasped and cried, "Oh my!
It's the most beautiful tail I've ever seen.
Go at once, and show it to the queen!"
The queen was astounded; she thanked the mermaid so
And returned the mermaid's tail, her face all aglow.
The mermaid happily went off on her way
And they all lived happily from that day.

PEARL'S WISDOM

Pearl had a garden
As pretty as can be.
As a five-year-old girl,
It filled her with glee.

She would run around the spacious,
Luscious, green grass.
She would sit among the flowers
And watch time pass.

The flowers were colourful,
And in full bloom;
She'd pick several bunches
To fill every room.

One day a wise old man
Walked by her house.
He wore a bright blue jacket.
(In the pocket was a mouse!)

He gave Pearl some seeds
And quietly said,
"Plant them over there,
In that flower bed."

"From the seeds, the tree of wisdom
Will surely grow.
From the tree you may take
What you need to know."

"But not a piece of wisdom
Is permitted to be seen
Until you have reached
The age of eighteen."

As the man walked away
Pearl said "Oh great!
But the age of eighteen?
That's so long to wait!"

Time passed by
And the tree slowly grew.
Its leaves, surprisingly,
Were a bright, bold blue.

One day Pearl sat alone
Feeling so bored.
By her parents,
She was being ignored.

She eyed the leaves
On her special tree.
I wonder, she thought,
What it can tell me.

Slowly but surely,
And secretly,
She picked a leaf
From the wisdom tree.

She looked carefully,
But not a thing it told her,
So she angrily tossed it
Over her shoulder.

She went to school
The very next day
And listened to what
Her teacher had to say.

She started to cry
And her chin hit the floor.
The things she had learned,
She knew no more.

She knew not one sum,
Not one number or letter,
And as the day passed,
It didn't get better.

What is happening to me?
What is going on?
Where are my lessons?
Where have they gone?

When she got home
The man came by,
Looked at the tree
And gave a mournful sigh.

"It seems you have betrayed
The wisdom tree," he said.
And for a long time,
He stood and shook his head.

"What do I do now?"
Pearl asked desperately.
"I didn't mean to betray
The special wisdom tree."

After a long pause,
The man began to speak
He said, "There just might be
Something we can tweak."

He walked around the tree,
Inspecting leaf by leaf.
"What you need," he said,
"Is a little belief."

"We can fix this thing,
Get you back on track;
All you need to do
Is get your knowledge back."

"But how? asked Pearl, quite puzzled.
"I think it's gone for good."
"Nonsense," said the man.
"We just need to search the wood."

So they headed to the forest,
Though Pearl knew not what for.
Suddenly they found a tree trunk
With a wooden door.

"Here it is," said the man.
"This is where we go."
He pushed open the door to see
A ground covered with snow.

A big expanse of snow,
With fir trees strong and tall.
"But how can this be?" said Pearl.
"The tree trunk is so small."

The man turned to face her
And softly tapped his nose.
He said "This is where
We find the man who knows."

They walked for what seemed
Miles and miles and miles,
Passing through all the gates
And climbing many stiles.

Finally, the man stopped
Right by a tower
And told Pearl that she needed
To find a magic flower.

Somehow she found a flower
Deep in the freezing snow.
It was red and white
With a magic, haunting glow.

They entered the tower
And there, they found a man
With a pointy blue hat
And a starry caftan.

"A wizard!" Pearl whispered,
Taking in the scene.
"Finally you come!" he said.
"Where have you been?"

Pearl and her companion
Explained their dilemma,
Pearl anxiously wondering,
If this man could help her.

"You know," the wizard said,
"What you did was very wrong.
But there's something you can do;
You need to sing a song:"

"Oh Wisdom Tree, oh Wisdom tree
So honest and so true,
Please grant me back my knowledge,
And I'll stay true to you."

"If you sing this song,
Every day for just a week,
Your knowledge will return
And things won't look so bleak."

"But to teach you a lesson
For the wrong you have done,
You cannot use the tree
Until the age of twenty one."

The man and Pearl agreed
That this was fair enough.
Pearl took it on the chin,
Although it would be tough.

A small price to pay
For her knowledge to return
And never again would she
Give in to such a yearn.

Pearl's knowledge did come back
When she sang to the tree.
Wisdom should never be toyed with.
Wouldn't you agree?

MY TRANSPARENT FRIEND

I had a little friend; he had transparent fur.
He flashed all different colours and had a deafening purr.
This funny little creature had free run of our house.
He was smaller than a tabby cat, but bigger than a mouse.
He could change his colours according to his mood,
If he was feeling threatened or simply wanted food.
He liked changing to tiger stripes and florescent yellow.
He turned a shade of dark grey when he was feeling mellow.
Sometimes he was a mixture of all his favourite creatures.
I think it's fair to say, it was one of his best features.
One day a strange man entered our grounds.
So silently he crept and skulked around.
He was going to treat us all like fools;
He was going to steal some very fine jewels.
Just in the nick of time, our friend sprung into action.
He was going to cause a dramatic distraction.
He turned a mixture of bright yellow and pink
And towards our intruder, he began to slink.
The man didn't spot our special pet approaching.
On the man's grand plan, he was encroaching.
The intruder reached the room that was filled with jewels.
It was locked so he needed his very best tools.
But as he reached for his tool box he heard
Something go, "tweet, tweet, tweet" like a bird.
That was followed by an ear-splitting roar
And straight after that, a crow's "caw, caw."
Our intruder turned around and what did he see?
Our pet standing there, oh so casually,
With fur bright pink and fluorescent yellow.
Shaking, the intruder said, "Hey there fellow."
Our pet gave one last almighty roar.
The intruder fled through our back door.
Our special pet had saved the day;
He'd frightened that nasty intruder away.
What a dear little pet; we treasured him so.
It was safe to say we'd never let him go.

BEHIND THE DOOR

They climbed the stone steps
To the big brown door.
What was behind it?
They wanted to explore.

A tree with purple leaves
Was shedding for Fall
What a strange tree!
It intrigued them all.

They knocked on the door;
There came no reply.
Was anyone in there?
They gave it one more try.

There was still no answer.
What should they do?
Try and open it, perhaps?
Would they walk straight through?

The door was stiff;
It stood solid and still.
To make it budge
Would take some skill.

But what was that noise?
The strange creaking sound?
Would someone let them in?
Could they look around?

Finally the door opened
And a voice said, "Come in!
We've been waiting for you.
Shall we begin?"

BEHIND THE DOOR II

They pushed the door wide open
And slowly wandered in;
They saw a bright red throne
And on that throne there sat a king.

He looked so very jolly,
A wide beam on his face.
"So you're my entertainers,"
He said, "Come and take your place."

"I'm sorry," said the leader.
"There must be some mistake.
We're not your entertainers.
You're a few centuries too late."

"Nonsense," said the king.
"There must be something you can do."
"Perhaps," said the group leader,
"We can find some tapping shoes."

They rummaged and they rummaged
Through every golden chest
In hope that they'd find something
To fulfil this quirky quest.

After hours of searching,
They found some fine costumes.
They decided to perform
In the king's fancy ballroom.

The king was so delighted;
He really was impressed.
He declared to this fine group,
"You have surely passed this test."

After a fine performance,
They gave one final bow.
The group leader said to the king,
"We must be going now."

Said the king, "I will not keep you.
You clearly have to go.
Be sure to visit me one day;
I'd love another show."

AS WE WATCHED THE FAIRIES DANCE

As we watched the fairies dance,
My brother and I,
We gave a happy
And wistful sigh.

As we watched them circle
Around and around,
We felt so very tall,
So far from the ground.

As we witnessed the dance,
We couldn't help but grin.
We really, truly wished
That we could join in.

So the next time we attended
A family celebration,
We danced in a circle
With such jubilation.

LOVABLE CHARACTERS

THE TOOTH FAIRY

She uses fairy magic to find your house;
She's tinier than the tiniest mouse.
She wears a white dress and has a pink wand;
Her eyes are ocean blue, and her hair, flowing blonde.
Being careful not to wake you, she flies up to your bed
And lands upon the pillow where you rest your sleepy head.
Using fairy magic, she swiftly takes your goods,
Which she'll take to her fairy friends, deep in the woods.
She leaves a golden coin from her box of fairy treasure.
This simple act gives her no end of pleasure.
Then oh so silently, she flies into the night,
Knowing that what you'll find will fill you with delight.

THE FAIRY DRAGON

The fairy dragon lives
In a house so enchanted.
Her powers should never
Be taken for granted.

She'll grant every wish
That the fairy folk make
While she sits all alone
By the magical lake.

But how does she feel
As she sits there alone?
Does she get lonely
Sitting all on her own,

Without a companion,
A playmate, a friend?
How much time alone
Does she spend?

Does she have friends
Who visit each day?
Do they splash in the lake
And laugh and play?

The fairies must love her
As she is so kind.
A more loving fairy friend
They could not find.

DR. A BLAKE

On the edge of a forest,
Sitting on the lake,
Is the luxurious home
Of Dr. A Blake.

An eccentric character
Who lives all alone
Among children and creatures,
His quirks are well known.

He wanders the woods
And everyone stares.
They say he eats snakes;
They say he traps bears.

But what it is
They don't know to be true
Is that he gets frightened
Just like me and you.

And as he watches
The days begin and end,
What he wishes for
Is to have a friend.

GENTLE GIANT

I am a gentle giant;
I live in Giant Town.
I tell the children stories;
I can calm them down.

I am a gentle giant;
I live in a giant house
With my giant ginger cat
And my friendly giant mouse.

I am a gentle giant;
I sit in a giant chair
With my giant food,
Which I just love to share.

I am a gentle giant.
Please don't be alarmed.
Come to Giant town and
To meet you, I'll be charmed.

THE FAIRY QUEEN

The fairy queen sits
On a purple throne of feathers.
She sits out and guards
The kingdom in all weathers.

She is bossy and bold,
But gentle and kind.
When you speak to her,
Your manners, you should mind.

She has long, dark hair
Filled with curls and waves.
She has a few faithful workers;
She doesn't take slaves.

If you feel like a visit
To her humble land,
You can bring a spade
To find treasures in the sand.

But leave them where you find them,
For she will always know;
If someone steals a treasure,
Her jewels will start to glow.

THE ICE FAIRY

On a vast snowy plain,
With one lone tree,
Lives a fairy,
As lonely as can be.

She is the ice fairy;
She wanders alone.
Nobody wants to
Visit her home.

They say she is cold
And not very nice.
They say that her heart
Is frozen like ice.

Would you be the one
To visit her home,
To see the places
She does roam?

Would you be the one
To befriend her,
And bring her a coat
All covered in fur?

Maybe the fairy
Isn't so bad.
Maybe she's feeling
Ever so sad.

So maybe go forth
To visit her home;
Go and make sure
She isn't alone.

THE ANGEL OF THE OAK TREE

The angel of the oak tree
Keeps those you love from harm.
When there's no rhyme or reason,
He holds us safe in arms.

The angel of the oak tree,
He has so many powers.
He's sitting near you as
You wile away the hours.

The angel of the oak tree,
He sees you on your way.
He listens to your dreams
And to everything you say.

PURPLE TIGER

There was a purple tiger
Who roamed a purple world,
Owned by a rich young lady
Who had a little girl.

They had a thousand servants
To tend the purple yard,
But the purple tiger was
The girl's own personal guard.

Protecting her from evil,
He followed her each day,
Making sure that no harm
Would ever come her way.

He got his magic powers
From a purple pond.
He didn't have the paws that
Could wave a magic wand.

Every single morning he
Would drink the magic water
And then he would return
To the owner's quarters.

And how the young girl loved him,
As did her mother too.
Would you like a tiger friend
To love and protect you?

THE GIANT CAT

As the fairies dwell
Among the long grass,
Skipping and playing
And watching time pass,

A giant cat
Explores the land;
Ginger and stripy,
Almighty and grand.

As he wanders
Towards the river,
The frightened fairies
Shake and quiver.

They hide among
Dandelion clocks,
Disguise themselves
With daisy frocks.

And if they can,
They hide away
In a giant
Bale of hay,

The giant cat,
He never sees
The fairies crouching
On their knees.

The fairies hope
That, one sweet day,
The giant cat
Will go away.

DRAGON IN A BOTTLE

I'm a dragon in a bottle.
I sit grandly all day.
I'm happy when the sun shines.
But not when clouds are grey.

I'm a dragon in a bottle.
I munch on purple leaves.
With my fearsome roar,
I scare away the thieves.

I'm a dragon in a bottle,
But I don't breathe fire.
Instead I sing more sweetly
Than a gospel choir.

I'm a dragon in a bottle.
Hear me when I say,
I love to see the world from here
Every single day.

ENCHANTED SETTINGS

UNDER THE BRIDGE

In the green forest,
Trees in full leaf
Surround a stone bridge;
But who dwells beneath?

On the clear waters
Of the cool lake,
Flowers float peacefully,
White and opaque.

Underneath the bridge,
Where darkness prevails,
Dwell strange, green creatures
With light blue tails.

They seek their food
All through the night;
And then, in the day,
They vanish from sight.

So if you cross the bridge,
You can have a peep.
But be sure to tiptoe
In case they're asleep.

THE WISHING WELL

In a hidden forest glade,
Many a wish a day is made,
And the one who promises not to tell
Is the magical, wooden wishing well.

People come from miles away,
Even when the skies are grey.
They walk along the winding path,
Filled with hope and not with wrath.

Until they reach the glade, so green
And the lushest grass they've ever seen.
With care, they approach the well
And their greatest wish they tell.

As the crystal water is glistening,
They pray that the well is listening.
And then they seek adventures new
In hope that, one day, their wish comes true.

MAGIC FOREST

There was a magic forest
With glittered trees and flowers,
Where fairies often wandered
To wile away the hours.

There was a magic forest
With fireflies all around,
Where flower fairies sang;
Such a warm and welcome sound!

There was a magic forest
Where white wizards appeared
And performed their magic show.
'Twas the best part of the year.

There was a magic forest
A long, long time ago.
But sadly it's a place
Where folk no longer go.

TREE OF SECRETS

Inside a tree trunk filled with light,
The tree of secrets is here tonight.

It only comes in Winter, never in Spring,
Nor Summer, nor Autumn, but here's the thing;

You tell it your secrets; it keeps them at bay.
It scares the demons and monsters away.

You get such a feeling of sweet release.
You walk away and you live in peace.

So look for the tree trunk all filled with light
And let all your secrets be free tonight.

ENCHANTED HOME

In a little enchanted home,
In a clearing where faires roam,
There is magic, there's mystery
And a true sense of history.

In a miniature enchanted abode,
In the woodland, far from the road,
Bright blue butterflies flutter about;
Wonder is everywhere, without a doubt.

In a dinky enchanted house
Live several fairies and a tiny mouse.
They live together in harmony,
With a magical spell, or two or three.

PURPLE FAIRY DOOR

When you open the purple fairy door
You will come to a place you'll want to explore.
There's so much to do to pass the hours;
You can sit among the pretty flowers;
You can speak to a fairy and make a wish;
You can ask the elf chef to make your favourite dish;
You can sing to the birds and they'll sing back to you.
There's a magical mountain with a never-ending view.
When you come through, you'll want to stay all day,
In the enchanted garden, where the fairies play.

THE ROYAL CASTLE

In a grey, stone castle,
In an enchanted yard,
The cooks and servants
Are working very hard.

The king and queen sit
On a throne of jewels,
Making sure their people
Are keeping to the rules.

While in the castle yard,
The grass grows lush green.
It must grow wild and free,
As ordered by the queen.

The two rocks that lie
Near the archway of trees
Make good meeting place
For the buzzy bees.

And when you see the toadstool,
The king and queen declare,
You must be very careful,
As fairies might dwell there.

STREAM

Down the forest steam
Wonders can be found;
A magical place
Where you'll hear the sound
Of fairies whispering
In the summer breeze,
Of elves spring cleaning
And scrubbing on their knees.
Walk along the stream;
Mind out for the prickles,
And you might just feel
Tiny fairy tickles.

STEPS IN THE WOOD

Will you climb the steps in the wood?
Will you stand where brave fairies stood?
Deep in the forest they did roam;
Deep in the forest was their home.

They would roam the forest in the night;
They would roam, giving goblins a fright.
The goblins were a terrible threat.
The goblins, they caused terrible fret.

They liked to destroy all things in their way.
They liked to destroy; it was their form of play.
The fairies were where their weakness laid;
For, of the fairies, they were afraid.

So when you climb the steps in the wood,
When you stand where the fairies stood,
Remember the courage the fairies showed.
Remember the debt the fairies are owed.

GLASS BALL

What if you could step
Into a little glass ball
And enter a forest,
The most magical of all?

What if you could shrink
To a miniature size?
Would you be in
For a pleasant surprise?

Would there be fairies
For you to meet?
Would there be fruit,
Succulent and sweet?

What if you could step
Into a little glass ball?
Would you possibly be
The luckiest of all?

ACKNOWLEDGEMENT

As always, I would like to thank my wonderful family and friends, who always support me in my work. Thank you, especially, for interacting with my posts on Social Media. It really means a lot to me and also allows my posts to be seen by more people, which ultimately helps my growth.

Thank you to my amazing husband, Dan, my biggest supporter and my best friend. You are always there with honest feedback and fantastic advice. You are my world.

I would also like thank my two lovely sons. You are my energy and every day you give me a reason to be proud. May you always chase your dreams.

To my wonderful community on Instagram, (You know who you are.) What can I say? Your support has been amazing. Your love and interaction has helped me to grow and develop from the writer I was when I first started writing poetry to the writer I am today. Thank you from the bottom of my heart.

And finally, thank you to my readers for buying this book and my previous books. I hope you have enjoyed reading my work.

ABOUT THE AUTHOR

Jen Elvy

Jen works in education and lives in Kent with her husband and two young sons. She loves writing poetry where her readers can escape to a fantasy world.

Her previous poetry collection, The Perfect Prompt, was written to inspire others to create and although there are no specific prompts in this book, she hopes that some or all of the poems can inspire your creativity.

BOOKS BY THIS AUTHOR

The Perfect Prompt

A collection of poems to inspire your creativity.

A Hunt For Sparkled Treasures

This is the first narrative poem in this book in ebook format

Printed in Great Britain
by Amazon